W9-BEB-330

The Biggest Animal Ever

By Allan Fowler

Consultants:

Robert L. Hillerich, Ph.D., Bowling Green State University, Bowling Green, Ohio

Mary Nalbandian, Director of Science, Chicago Public Schools, Chicago, Illinois

Fay Robinson, Child Development Specialist

SCHOLASTIC INC.

New York Toronto London Auckland Sydney
Mexico City New Delhi Hong Kong Buenos Aires

Design by Beth Herman Design Associates

No part of this publication may be reproduced in whole or in part,
or stored in a retrieval system, or transmitted in any form or by any means,
electronic, mechanical, photocopying, recording, or otherwise, without written
permission of the publisher. For information regarding permission, write to
Permissions Department, Grolier Incorporated, a subsidiary of Scholastic Inc.,
90 Old Sherman Turnpike, Danbury, CT 06816.

ISBN 0-516-24519-8

12 11 10 9 8 7   4 5 6 7/0

Printed in the U.S.A.   10

First Scholastic printing, September 2002

Do you know which animal is the biggest one ever?

It's an animal alive today —
the blue whale.

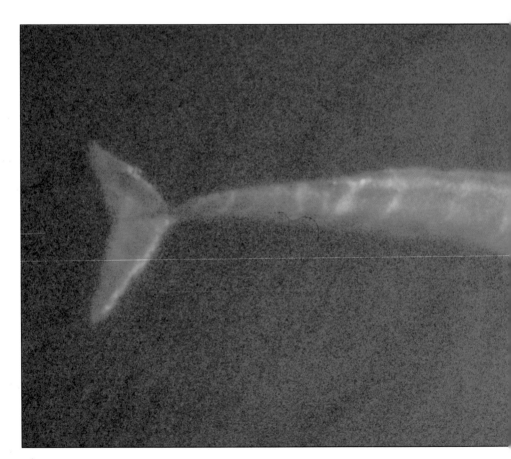

This animal weighs
more than the biggest
dinosaur that ever lived.

Whales are mammals, even
though they look like fish.

Dogs and cats, horses and elephants — people, too — are mammals.

Like almost all mammals, baby whales are born from their mother's body, not from eggs.

A baby whale is called a calf. It feeds on milk from its mother's body.

And like all mammals,
whales breathe air.

A whale can stay
underwater a long time.

But it must come up to the surface to breathe.

When you see whales spout, they are breathing. They blow out the old air through a blowhole on top of their head.

16

Whales are among the smartest animals.

They can hear underwater.

It is possible that they hear sounds from hundreds of miles away.

Whales whistle, grunt, and sing to each other.

Scientists have studied these whale "songs."

Are whales talking? Well, they seem to understand each other!

19

Dolphins and porpoises are
very much like whales.

They are very friendly
and love to play.

At marine parks, you can
see dolphins leap high out
of the water.

Not too long ago, whales were hunted and killed. People wanted oil from the whales to burn in lamps.

But the hunters killed too many whales. Some kinds of whales were almost lost forever.

Now there are laws to protect whales from harm.

There are boats that take
people where they can
learn about whales without
bothering them.

The biggest animal that ever lived deserves our best care.

Words You Know

whales

blue whale

breathing

blowhole

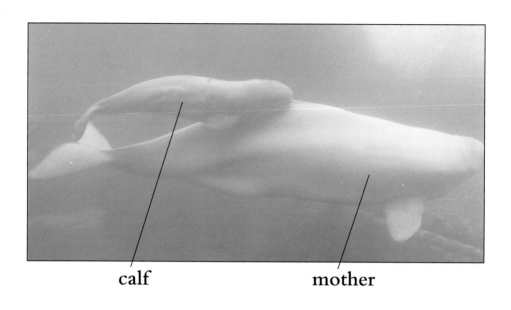

calf   mother

dolphin   mammal

Index

About the Author

Allan Fowler is a free-lance writer with a background in advertising. Born in New York, he lives in Chicago now and enjoys traveling.

Photo Credits

A/P Wide World Photos – ©Ed Baily, 8, 31 (top)

marine mammal images – ©Mark Conlin, 6

PhotoEdit – ©Myrleen Ferguson, 7, 31 (bottom right)

Jeff Rotman Photography – ©Bob Cranston, 11; ©Itamar Grinberg, 20

©1992 Sea World of Florida – 22, 31 (bottom left)

SuperStock International, Inc. – 24, 25

Valan – ©Richard Sears, Cover, 4-5, 12, 15, 28, 30 (3 photos);
©Kennon Cooke, 9, 21; ©Fred Bruemmer, 16; ©Jeff Foote, 19, 26, 27;
©Francis Lépine, 23

COVER: Blue Whale